5. What did the World Wide Web Consortium try to establish?
A. a Do Not Track standard
B. uniform privacy policy guidelines
C. uniform opt-in requirements
D. the e-privacy directive

6. Which of the following are most likely the least impacted by the Fair and Accurate Credit Transactions Act?
A. consumer reporting agencies
B. government agencies
C. employers
D. identity theft committees

7. What can be considered an issue when tort law and state law provide employee privacy protection?
A. there needs to be flagrant disregard for privacy
B. torts cannot be relied on in an employment context
C. dismissal is unavoidable, due to employment at will
D. it can be difficult to determine jurisdiction

8. Which of the following concerns practices that misrepresent the true intention?
A. the Fair and Accurate Credit Transactions Act
B. the Fair Credit Reporting Act
C. section 5 of the Federal Trade Commission Act
D. the Dodd-Frank Act

9. Regarding civil liability, which of the following is most likely true?
A. liberty and freedom are not at stake
B. there is a heavier burden of proof than for criminal cases
C. guilt must be beyond and to the exclusion of a reasonable doubt
D. penalties are high

10. What is the leaving out of certain medical details ?
A. Personal Health Information restriction
B. redaction
C. privacy concern restriction
D. editing

This case should be used for the following three questions:
A website called "Parentpresents" allows children of all ages to order gifts that adults like, to make their parents happy. Kids can visit the website, provide minimal input as to their parents' preferences, and a gift is selected without revealing the content to the child that orders the gift.
Of course there is a return policy, as ordering an unknown gift carries with it the risk that the parent already owns an item that is part of the gift. All address details are kept for several months, which is how long the return policy for unopened items is valid. The website also uses a tracking pixel, to link the visitors to social media profiles. This is done in an effort to map the customer base as well as provide targeted advertisement to children from similar areas and with similar interests.

11. What could the website do to comply with the Children's Online Privacy Protection Act?
A. a Children's Online Privacy Protection Act compliance code
B. Federal Communications Commission approval
C. Federal Trade Commission supervision
D. a consent decree

If you have just spent $550 purchasing the CIPP/US exam, and another $250 for the membership fee or maintenance fee, you will probably want to practice before taking the exam using a practice exam that comes as close to the real exam as possible. This document contains that practice exam, with questions that trick you into choosing the wrong answer, vague phrasing and all the other misleading things you can expect on exam day. Be warned: this practice exam will frustrate you, as will the CIPP/US exam. However, if you put in the effort and build up the tolerance towards the frustrating questions, you will pass the exam.

Using this document you will learn to: 1. read questions thoroughly and think about what exactly is asked; 2. deal with the frustration of questions that have multiple correct or all incorrect answers; 3. time yourself, making the most out of the exam's review option; 4. learn to gamble on questions that contain information not covered by your study material; 5. test your knowledge of the subject matter.

This document contains 90 questions, like the actual exam. Take 2.5 hours to complete it and if you fully understand the correct options after reading the explanations, you are ready to schedule your exam. At the end of the document there is an answer key, as well as more information for each question that explains the logic of the question or provides a little more information on the subject of the question.

Good luck!

EXAM QUESTIONS

1. How can spam in the context of the Controlling the Assault of Non-Solicited Pornography And Marketing Act best be described?
A. unsolicited mail
B. erotic, political or religious e-mails
C. unwanted e-mail messages sent to a large number of people
D. undesired transactional or relationship e-mails

2. Which of the following does management and administration of personal information not include?
A. defining accountability
B. penalization
C. assigning accountability
D. documenting accountability

3. In which of the following specific areas is a Federal law in place that provides workplace privacy to a certain extent?
A. prohibiting discrimination
B. restroom surveillance
C. allowing e-mail access
D. listening in on phone calls

4. What is an example of self-regulation?
A. the Organisation for Economic Co-operation and Development guidelines
B. the Fair Information Practices
C. the PCI DSS
D. the General Data Protection Regulation

12. In this case, which of the following is most true regarding children's privacy?
A. the Federal Trade Commission has specific authority
B. the Federal Trade Commission has general authority
C. the Federal Communications Office has specific authority
D. the Federal Communications Commission has general authority

13. How is the tracking pixel also frequently called?
A. functional cookie
B. session cookie
C. permanent cookie
D. web beacon

14. Which of the following statements is most appropriate concerning international exchange students?
A. the Family Educational Rights and Privacy Act is the strictest applicable law
B. foreign exchange students are not covered by the Family Educational Rights and Privacy Act
C. foreign exchange students can enjoy a higher level of protection
D. medical treatment records fall out of the Family Educational Rights and Privacy Act's scope

15. What would be the most likely reason for implementing a privacy program?
A. ensure full compliance
B. train employees
C. increasing the organization's ability to comply with privacy laws
D. required by the Federal Trade Commission

16. In the context of data retention and disposal, which of the following is true?
A. the Health Insurance Portability and Accountability Act contains retention and disposal requirements
B. the Children's Online Privacy Protection Act contains retention and disposal requirements
C. the Fair and Accurate Credit Transactions Act contains retention and disposal requirements
D. Cable Communications Policy Act contains retention and disposal requirements

17. As a privacy officer, which law would you familiarize yourself with when your organization opens a location in South Africa?
A. the General Data Protection Regulation
B. the CLOUD Act
C. the Personal Information Protection and Electronic Documents Act
D. the Protection Of Personal Information Act

18. Which of the following organizations would most likely require an auditable incident response plan?
A. all organizations that accept payment cards
B. organizations handling medical data
C. credit reporting agencies
D. multinational organizations in the European Union

19. When would an organization join Privacy SHIELD (if still valid)?
A. when expanding business to South Africa
B. when expanding business to Europe
C. when expanding business to Canada
D. when expanding business to South America

20. How did the essay "The Right To Privacy" define privacy?
A. password protected e-mails
B. uninterrupted communication
C. shielding from harm
D. the right to be let alone

21. Which of the following most likely protects against deceptive trade practices?
A. a consent decree
B. not selling customer data
C. well trained personnel
D. an accurate privacy notice

22. If an organization sells to customers internationally, which of the following is the most important privacy-related point of attention?
A. the knowledge regarding foreign legislation of the privacy advisor
B. which countries are actually targeted
C. the CLOUD Act and its consequences for international personal information handling
D. whether the Fourth Amendment has any impact

23. Which of the following is the least true regarding the Asia-Pacific Economic Cooperation privacy framework?
A. the Asia-Pacific Economic Cooperation privacy framework can aid in determining security safeguards
B. the Asia-Pacific Economic Cooperation privacy framework is meant to describe accountability
C. the Asia-Pacific Economic Cooperation privacy framework intends to prevent harm
D. the Asia-Pacific Economic Cooperation privacy framework intends to restrict the use of personal information

24. The Gramm-Leach-Bliley Act contains a requirement for which of the following?
A. the creation of a data inventory
B. a written plan on incident response
C. the requirement for a procedure to handle security incidents
D. compliance with state breach notification statutes

25. Which of the following is the best example of territorial privacy?
A. security guards screening people that enter a venue
B. privacy arranged per country
C. restricted areas requiring authorization to enter
D. video surveillance

26. If a data breach occurs, which of the following would you advise as a Privacy Officer?
A. tell the Chief Executive Officer to hire a Chief Information Security Officer
B. inform all persons whose personal information was involved
C. delete the encryption key used for all personal information
D. create an inventory of broken barriers

27. Which of the following is the most appropriate description of Big Data?
A. complex and large datasets
B. files of several Gigabytes
C. sensitive files
D. a dataset containing information on extremely different individuals

28. What is the biggest advantage of a consent decree for individuals?
A. there is no explicit admission of guilt
B. there is no implicit admission of guilt
C. the alleged violation is stopped
D. an investigation is started in case of a suspected violation of the consent decree

29. Which of the following most accurately describes the principal mission of the Federal Trade Commission?
A. the protection of consumers and limiting the use of personal information
B. assist the president in the regulation of privacy practices
C. promotion of the consumer protection and elimination of anticompetitive practices
D. enforce legislation on a national and state level

This case should be used for the following two questions:
A cloud provider rents out terabytes of cheap storage space, with regular virus scans on the files that are stored. Customers love the service, because it makes them feel safe and they think the virus scanning results in files that are clean and unable to do any damage.
Renting storage space is easy and there is no need to provide identification when setting up an account. Payment can be made by money order or credit card. The cloud provider also declares, in its privacy notice, that only the user is able to access the files. Then, as can be expected, the police contact the cloud provider inquiring about the data one of its users has uploaded. This specific person is part of a murder investigation, and his data may prove to be useful evidence. The police would like access.

30. What would the police need in order for the cloud provider to provide them with access?
A. a court order
B. a compelling case
C. an exception under the General Data Protection Regulation
D. a data qualification

31. What can be said about the situation if the cloud provider were to provide the police with immediate access, without further requirements?
A. it is reasonable to expect law enforcement to have unconditional access to the files in case of a crime
B. the cloud provider is never obliged to cooperate
C. this would constitute a breach of the privacy statement
D. the cloud provider is obliged to cooperate

32. Which of the following statements is most accurate regarding the Children's Online Privacy Protection Act?
A. all websites potentially target children and require implementation
B. whether or not a privacy notice or statement is in place can result in deceptive practices
C. de-identified data is still within scope, if the child is below 13 years of age
D. for websites targeting children 12 years and younger, the Children's Online Privacy Protection Act applies

33. Who publishes and maintains the Federal Communication Commission's official rules?
A. the Government Printing Office
B. the Federal Trade Commission
C. the Department of Education
D. the Federal District Court

34. Which of the following is not one of the four categories of the Fair Information Practices?
A. right of deletion
B. control of the information
C. information lifecycle
D. information management

35. What recommendation would you give as a privacy officer, to prevent leaking personal information?
A. storing data de-identified
B. storing data aggregated
C. encryption of data with 256-bit encryption
D. storing files compressed

36. How is the Health Insurance Portability and Accountability Act also known?
A. the Health Information Technology for Economic and Clinical Health Act
B. the Electronic Transactions Act
C. the Kennedy-Kassebaum Act
D. the Clinton Health Act

37. After requesting access, how many days does an organization have to provide a copy of Personal Health Information?
A. sixty days
B. twenty days
C. twenty five days
D. thirty days

38. What was the most likely reason for the Confidentiality of Substance Use Disorder Patient Records Rule?
A. to ensure that patients do not face adverse consequences
B. widening circumstances of disclosure, while increasing safeguards
C. mandating fully documented parental consent, regardless of the age of the patient
D. prevention of disclosure of patient information

39. Which of the following is covered by Title I of the Health Insurance Portability and Accountability Act?
A. guidelines for group health plans
B. guidelines for pre-tax medical spending accounts
C. workers and their families
D. administrative simplification procedures

40. Which of the following was most likely not a concern with the Health Insurance Portability and Accountability Act?
A. the increase in paperwork
B. the penalties
C. the data security requirements
D. the implementation workload

41. What is most likely true regarding the Health Insurance Portability and Accountability Act in the context of research?
A. there is a decrease in follow-up surveys
B. the de-identification requirements of the Health Insurance Portability and Accountability Act privacy rule are impractical
C. informed consent forms are even required for de-identified data
D. the layered privacy notice requirement has hindered data collection

42. Of the following, which doesn't preempt state law in most areas?
A. the Fair and Accurate Credit Transactions Act
B. the Children's Online Privacy Protection Act
C. the Health Insurance Portability and Accountability Act
D. the Controlling the Assault of Non-Solicited Pornography And Marketing Act

43. What is needed for a potential employer when requesting a consumer report?
A. employee consent
B. certifying for permissible purposes
C. a General Data Protection Regulation legal basis
D. a reluctant potential employee

44. Which of the following requires that debit card numbers are not fully visible?
A. the General Data Protection Regulation
B. the Health Insurance Portability and Accountability Act
C. the Fair and Accurate Credit Transaction Act
D. no law requires anything like this

45. Which of the following requires disposal of consumer reports?
A. Equifax
B. TransUnion
C. the disposal rule
D. the Federal Communications Commission

46. Which is true about the Red Flags Rule?
A. anyone lending money is covered by the Red Flags rule
B. the Red Flags Rule applies to a broad list of businesses
C. anyone borrowing money is covered
D. it allows victims to recover the costs

47. What was the biggest issue in the case of U.S. Bancorp?
A. the credit card data of its customers was stored unencrypted, including the CCV number
B. outsourcing to Asia without consumer awareness
C. no actual security issue, but the sharing of customer information
D. a Children's Online Privacy Protection Act violation

48. Which of the following most accurately describes a criminal trial?
A. greater weight of the evidence counts
B. the burden of proof lies with the defendant
C. settles a dispute
D. liberty and freedom of an individual are at stake

49. What is the most true about the Family Educational Rights and Privacy Act?
A. high school students must consent to sharing their personal information
B. state university students must consent to sharing their personal information
C. parents have an absolute right to the personal information of their children
D. parents can prevent deletion of a student's personal information

50. Which is most true regarding the US National Do Not Call Registry?
A. after your number is on the registry for 31 days, you can report unwanted sales calls
B. random dialing by non-humans circumvents the Do Not Call Registry
C. the Do Not Call Registry needs to be refreshed every 31 days
D. the Do Not Call Registry does not protect against robocalls

51. Which Act is complied with, with the Do Not Call Registry?
A. the Do-Not-Call Implementation Act
B. the Telephone Consumer Protection Act
C. the Do-Not-Call Improvement Act
D. the Federal Trade Commission Act

52. Which of the following is true regarding telemarketing?
A. in certain states, the Do Not Call Registry can be ignored
B. whenever a call is made, consent must be clear and conspicuous
C. calls can only be made between 12 am and 3 pm
D. calls can only be made between 10 am and 3 pm

53. What is common in most definitions of personal information?
A. it refers to medical information
B. it concerns large groups of people
C. it is sensitive
D. it is information about a person

54. Which of the following is not one of the three basic types of compliance under the Controlling the Assault of Non-Solicited Pornography And Marketing Act?
A. unsubscribe compliance
B. notice compliance
C. content compliance
D. sending behavior compliance

55. Which state added an explicit guarantee of privacy to its constitution in 1972?
A. New York
B. Washington
C. California
D. North Carolina

56. Which of the following contains a requirement for the redaction of sensitive personal information?
A. the Health Information Technology for Economic and Clinical Health Act
B. the Federal Rules of Civil Procedure
C. the Health Insurance Portability and Accountability Act
D. New York state law

57. Which of the following is not true regarding information in the Federal Rule of Civil Procedure 45?
A. production of documents can be commanded, including electronically stored information
B. a person responding to a subpoena can be required to label the requested documents
C. photographic evidence of the receipt of the subpoena is required
D. a person commanded to produce documents does not always have to appear at the place of production

58. Which of the following fits a protective order in the context of personal information?
A. a protective order protects only the victims during a criminal case
B. a protective order protects only the defendant in a civil case
C. a protective order is often issued to protect against unreasonable discovery requests
D. a protective order prevents information to ever become known to the public

59. How does the Third Amendment provide privacy protection?
A. allows defendants to remain silent
B. prevents soldiers from entering a person's home
C. prevents selective witness selection
D. limits freedom of speech

60. Which of the following is least likely applicable during e-discovery?
A. redaction requirements
B. mandated publication
C. protective orders
D. confidentiality protections

61. Which law from 1361 called for the arrest of peeping Toms?
A. the Fourth Amendment
B. the Justices of Peace Act
C. the Farm Goods Distribution Act
D. the Digital Telephony Act

62. Which of the following was the biggest issue in the Nomi case?
A. Nomi collected MAC addresses of its clients' mobile devices
B. Nomi misled customers
C. Nomi generated and sold analytics reports about its customers' retail traffic
D. Nomi did not adequately protect the personal information it stored

63. What can most significantly change the level of privacy protection of an employment at will situation?
A. a contract
B. a criminal case
C. a civil case
D. a consent decree

64. Of the following, which is the earliest stage of employee privacy protection?
A. employment drug test
B. CCTV in the lobby
C. consumer reports
D. a polygraph test

65. What is created by section 217 of the USA PATRIOT Act?
A. the establishment of the Federal Trade Commission's authorization
B. the computer trespasser exception
C. the establishment of the Federal Bureau of Investigation's authorization
D. the obligation of employers to aid in terrorism investigation

66. What would you recommend as a privacy officer if an organization wants to determine what protection to apply to which data?
A. Data inventory
B. Data classification
C. Data flow
D. encryption requirements

67. What can be said about comprehensive privacy laws in the US?
A. except for the Children's Online Privacy Protection Act, there is no comprehensive privacy law
B. the Health Insurance Portability and Accountability Act is partially comprehensive, but does not preempt state law
C. the General Data Protection Regulation is the only comprehensive privacy law
D. the privacy laws that do not preempt state law are not comprehensive

68. Which of the following is least likely an incentive for collecting data on employees?
A. European Union legislation in the case of international data transfers
B. safe workplace practices
C. preventing negligence
D. compliance with labor laws

69. In an international organization, which of the following is most likely true?
A. employees from the European Union seconded in the US could be entitled to the same level of protection as in the European Union
B. the Personal Information Protection and Electronic Documents Act applies to US & Canada government collaborations
C. for an organization from the European Union, European Union legislation applies to US employees in its US branch
D. India's IT law restricts employment practices in the US

70. Which of the following is not true regarding geo-location monitoring by employers in Connecticut?
A. $500 penalty for a first offence
B. a prior written notice needs to be provided
C. only monitoring practices from a specific exemption list are allowed
D. a civil penalty

71. Which of the following are partially exempt or not covered under the Employee Polygraph Protection Act?
A. security firms
B. pharmaceutical distributors
C. state government agencies
D. elementary schools

72. Of the following, which is least possibly leading to an obligation to provide personal information?
A. private investigations
B. civil litigation
C. criminal investigations
D. criminal litigation

73. In which context was the "reasonable expectation of privacy" test developed?
A. the Clinton administration
B. government wiretaps
C. the Obama administration
D. a consent decree

74. Which of the following was least likely the biggest issue in the snapchat case?
A. chats could be stored indefinitely
B. snapchat did not provide enough security
C. snapchat stored passwords non-hashed
D. hackers had access to a large number of user names and phone numbers

75. Which of the following is least likely considered a data breach incident?
A. an occurrence of hacking
B. the consequences of malware
C. stolen ciphertext
D. the loss of paper documents

76. Which of the following statements regarding data breaches is least likely true?
A. paper documents can possibly constitute a data breach
B. given its malicious nature, malware always results in a data breach
C. even an encrypted USB key can result in the requirement to inform the victims
D. the European Union's data breach reporting requirements are also applicable to US organizations

This case should be used for the following four questions:
A dating website with members all over the world has a unique matching algorithm that matches people based on facial features that have been scientifically proven to result in some form of compatibility. Users consent to the use of facial analysis and the creation of a profile.
Other than for the use of the website, the characteristics of the members that are gathered through the facial scans and conversations with other members, are also used for selling advertisement. Advertisers can buy advertisement space on the website, only visible to a person with a certain profile.
One day, a user is upset with the service, because all her dates have resulted in rejection. The frustration has led her to learn how to hack, and she has breached the website's security and stolen the database with profiles.

77. Which of the following statements is least likely true regarding the part of the dating website hosted in Europe and Hong Kong?
A. the General Data Protection Regulation will have implications for practices in the US
B. for Hong Kong, China's privacy laws are applicable
C. the Data Protection Officer from Europe will have full access to US practices
D. if there is no mixing of employees, the privacy practices can remain in place

78. Which is required for the users from the European Union for the processing of their sexual preference?
A. a contract
B. legitimate interest
C. consent
D. a privacy notice

79. Which of the following is most likely true about storing the political tendencies based on the analysis of someone's face for the members in Europe?
A. constitutes sensitive personal data
B. can be processed
C. political tendencies generated by the website are not personal data
D. political tendencies can be used without consent if not published

80. If the website is hosted in the European Union, what needs to happen after the breach?
A. a police investigation is required before reporting any breach
B. the breach needs to be reported to the Data Protection Authority
C. if personal data is accessed but not shared, no breach needs to be reported
D. the information security officer determined whether a breach needs to be reported

81. Regarding workplace privacy, and the monitoring of employees, which of the following is closest to being true?
A. employment at will extends to Europe and Asia due to US ownership, and the organization has more discretion over how to monitor workplace activity
B. if labor unions agree, workplace monitoring practices can be altered in Europe and Hong Kong
C. depending on the financial situation, workplace monitoring can be adapted to the means available
D. there is likely going to be a revision of workplace practices before they can be used in the European branch after a US company buys a company in the European Union

82. Which of the following statements regarding the different branches of government is most accurate?
A. the executive branch oversees the operational branch by means of the Federal Trade Commission and the Federal Communications Commission
B. the operational branch implements legislation created by the legislative branch
C. the judicial branch composes legislation that is voted on by the operational branch
D. the legislative branch votes on legislation before it is passed

83. If a website claims one thing regarding its processing of personal information, and then does another, what would this likely be called?
A. illegitimate processing
B. deceptive practice
C. publicity given to private life
D. unfair practice

84. Which of the following best describes a presidential veto?
A. the requirement for input from the president
B. the ability of the president to decide alone
C. the requirement for the president's signature
D. the ability to say no to a suggestion of congress

85. The Fair and Accurate Credit Transactions Act does not help with which of the following?
A. limiting the use of sharing
B. credit history restoration
C. limit the use of medical information
D. soliciting consumer input

86. When looking at the privacy laws in Canada, Europe and Asia, which class of privacy is most comprehensively protected?
A. bodily privacy
B. territorial privacy
C. information privacy
D. communications privacy

87. When looking at the Fair Information Practices, which of the following is not one of them?
A. notice
B. choice and consent
C. disclosure
D. supervision

88. Which of the following is true about robocalls?
A. they are only allowed to take place within certain hours
B. they are prerecorded
C. they can only take place if there is a pre-existing business relationship
D. a robot touches the dial

89. What cannot be said about common law?
A. it requires privacy torts
B. it is developed in case law
C. can draw on social customs
D. can draw on expectations

90. When would a privacy officer most likely recommend informing people of an updated privacy notice?
A. every year
B. when reaching a certain number of clients
C. when personal information will be handled differently
D. every month

ANSWER KEY
1A, 2B, 3A, 4C, 5A, 6B, 7A, 8C, 9A, 10B, 11A, 12A, 13D, 14C,
15C, 16C, 17D, 18A, 19B, 20D, 21D, 22B, 23D, 24C, 25D, 26D,
27A, 28C, 29C, 30A, 31C, 32D, 33A, 34A, 35A, 36C, 37D, 38A,
39C, 40C, 41A, 42C, 43B, 44C, 45C, 46B, 47C, 48D, 49B, 50A,
51A, 52B, 53D, 54B, 55C, 56B, 57C, 58C, 59B, 60B, 61B, 62B,
63A, 64C, 65B, 66B, 67D, 68A, 69A, 70C, 71D, 72A, 73B, 74C,
75C, 76B, 77B, 78C, 79A, 80B, 81D, 82D, 83B, 84D, 85D, 86C,
87D, 88B, 89A, 90C

EXPLANATIONS

1. How can spam in the context of the Controlling the Assault of Non-Solicited Pornography And Marketing Act best be described?
A. unsolicited mail
More information:
The word to look for here is unsolicited. All three other options do not make it evident that the messages are unsolicited.

2. Which of the following does management and administration of personal information not include?
B. penalization
More information:
Penalization is not part of the management and administration that is mentioned in your study material. It is to manage the violation, not the personal information.

3. In which of the following specific areas is a Federal law in place that provides workplace privacy to a certain extent?
A. prohibiting discrimination
More information:
There are several anti-discrimination laws (such as the Genetic Information Nondiscrimination Act) that forbid discrimination, and therefore take away some of the reasons for employers to collect certain information. If employers cannot make decisions based on the information, they are less likely to collect it.

4. What is an example of self-regulation?
C. the PCI DSS
More information:
The PCI DSS standards are standards composed by the payment card industry. Thus, self-regulation.

5. What did the World Wide Web Consortium try to establish?
A. a Do Not Track standard
More information:
As your study material will tell you, the World Wide Web Consortium tried to establish a Do Not Track standard.

6. Which of the following are most likely the least impacted by the Fair and Accurate Credit Transactions Act?
B. government agencies
More information:
Government agencies are not specifically impacted by the Fair and Accurate Credit Transactions Act. The others are specifically impacted.

7. What can be considered an issue when tort law and state law provide employee privacy protection?
A. there needs to be flagrant disregard for privacy
More information:
It can be difficult to prove that there was a privacy violation. Therefore, it will have to be significant and obvious to be able to prove it in court.

8. Which of the following concerns practices that misrepresent the true intention?
C. section 5 of the Federal Trade Commission Act
More information:
Section 5 of the Federal Trade Commission Act concerns unfair and deceptive acts or practices.

9. Regarding civil liability, which of the following is most likely true?
A. liberty and freedom are not at stake
More information:
During a civil case, liberty and freedom are likely not at stake and it is mostly to settle a dispute between two parties. Penalties could be high, but there is not necessarily a penalty, and whether something is high is subjective and hence something to be cautious about when choosing it as the correct answer.

10. What is the leaving out of certain medical details ?
B. redaction
More information:
Leaving out medical details is called redaction. See the Health Insurance Portability and Accountability Act for the scope of what can be redacted.

This case should be used for the following three questions:
A website called "Parentpresents" allows children of all ages to order gifts that adults like, to make their parents happy. Kids can visit the website, provide minimal input as to their parents' preferences, and a gift is selected without revealing the content to the child that orders the gift.
Of course there is a return policy, as ordering an unknown gift carries with it the risk that the parent already owns an item that is part of the gift. All address details are kept for several months, which is how long the return policy for unopened items is valid. The website also uses a tracking pixel, to link the visitors to social media profiles. This is done in an effort to map the customer base as well as provide targeted advertisement to children from similar areas and with similar interests.

11. What could the website do to comply with the Children's Online Privacy Protection Act?
A. a Children's Online Privacy Protection Act compliance code
More information:
To comply with the Children's Online Privacy Protection Act, a compliance code can be composed. This code contains the way in which an organization intends to be compliant.

12. In this case, which of the following is most true regarding children's privacy?
A. the Federal Trade Commission has specific authority
authority
More information:
The Federal Trade Commission has specific authority for the Children's Online Privacy Protection Act, which concerns children's privacy. Given the depth of your study materials, this is the most likely answer.

13. How is the tracking pixel also frequently called?
D. web beacon
More information:
A pixel placed on a website that tracks who visits the website is also referred to as a web beacon. Think of the facebook pixel, which allows the creation profiles of its users for advertisement purposes based on the visits to websites containing their web beacon.

14. Which of the following statements is most appropriate concerning international exchange students?
C. foreign exchange students can enjoy a higher level of protection
More information:
It can be the case that foreign exchange students enjoy a higher level of protection. If, for example, a US University targets students from the European Union for an exchange, the General Data Protection Regulation could apply or the European University requires the US University to sign a Data Processing Agreement in which the ways of dealing with personal information/data is specified.

15. What would be the most likely reason for implementing a privacy program?
C. increasing the organization's ability to comply with privacy laws
More information:
When implementing a privacy program, often a road map towards compliance is created at some point, which allows an organization to see what it needs to do to be compliant. This increases the organization's ability to comply with privacy laws.

16. In the context of data retention and disposal, which of the following is true?
C. the Fair and Accurate Credit Transactions Act contains retention and disposal requirements
More information:
The Fair and Accurate Credit Transactions Act contains retention and disposal requirements. The others contain only one or neither.

17. As a privacy officer, which law would you familiarize yourself with when your organization opens a location in South Africa?
D. the Protection Of Personal Information Act
More information:
The Protection Of Personal Information Act is a South African privacy law. This should be in your study materials if they are up-to-date.

18. Which of the following organizations would most likely require an auditable incident response plan?
A. all organizations that accept payment cards
More information:
The requirement referred to is mentioned in the Payment Card Industry Data Security Standards. There is no need to be completely familiar with these standards, but it is necessary to know that they exist and impose security requirements (such as an incident response plan).

19. When would an organization join Privacy SHIELD (if still valid)?
B. when expanding business to Europe
More information:
When an organization in the European Union wishes to transfer personal data to the US, one of the ways to do this without additional measures is if that organization joined Privacy SHIELD. Be careful though, things are likely to change.

20. How did the essay "The Right To Privacy" define privacy?
D. the right to be let alone
More information:
The essay "The Right to Privacy" defined privacy as the right to be let alone.

21. Which of the following most likely protects against deceptive trade practices?
D. an accurate privacy notice
More information:
If the privacy notice is accurate, it is clear for the reader what the organization will do with the personal information. Hence, no deception. The other options are not necessarily avoiding deception.

22. If an organization sells to customers internationally, which of the following is the most important privacy-related point of attention?
B. which countries are actually targeted
More information:
The first step here is to see which countries are targeted, as this can make a difference in the laws that apply. For example the General Data Protection Regulation applies if citizens from the European Union are targeted.

23. Which of the following is the least true regarding the Asia-Pacific Economic Cooperation privacy framework?
D. the Asia-Pacific Economic Cooperation privacy framework intends to restrict the use of personal information
More information:
The Asia-Pacific Economic Cooperation privacy framework is not intended to restrict the use of personal information. If at any point one of the answers contains the word "restrict" or a similar word, read it carefully. Privacy laws/frameworks/etc. are generally intended to protect and any possible restrictive effect was not the intention.

24. The Gramm-Leach-Bliley Act contains a requirement for which of the following?
C. the requirement for a procedure to handle security incidents
More information:
The Gramm-Leach-Bliley Act contains a procedure to handle security incidents. However, this does not have to be a written procedure.

25. Which of the following is the best example of territorial privacy?
D. video surveillance
More information:
Video surveillance invades a person's space, and hence likely constitutes territorial privacy.

26. If a data breach occurs, which of the following would you advise as a Privacy Officer?
D. create an inventory of broken barriers
More information:
Of the options presented, to see what went wrong is the best first step. After, it should be clear what went wrong and what the consequences are. After the cause and possible consequences are known, further action can be taken if needed.

27. Which of the following is the most appropriate description of Big Data?
A. complex and large datasets
individuals
More information:
Big Data is a term often used, and the best description of the options is complex and large datasets.

28. What is the biggest advantage of a consent decree for individuals?
C. the alleged violation is stopped
More information:
Individuals gain the most from the violation being stopped, since this will stop any actions with their personal information that negatively affects them.

29. Which of the following most accurately describes the principal mission of the Federal Trade Commission?
C. promotion of the consumer protection and elimination of anticompetitive practices
More information:
The principal mission of the Federal Trade Commission is the promotion of consumer protection and elimination of anticompetitive practices. Privacy violations can fall under this mission.

This case should be used for the following two questions:
A cloud provider rents out terabytes of cheap storage space, with regular virus scans on the files that are stored. Customers love the service, because it makes them feel safe and they think the virus scanning results in files that are clean and unable to do any damage.
Renting storage space is easy and there is no need to provide identification when setting up an account. Payment can be made by money order or credit card. The cloud provider also declares, in its privacy notice, that only the user is able to access the files. Then, as can be expected, the police contact the cloud provider inquiring about the data one of its users has uploaded. This specific person is part of a murder investigation, and his data may prove to be useful evidence. The police would like access.

30. What would the police need in order for the cloud provider to provide them with access?
A. a court order
More information:
Of the provided options, a court order is the most likely way the police can get the cloud provider to provide them with access.

31. What can be said about the situation if the cloud provider were to provide the police with immediate access, without further requirements?
C. this would constitute a breach of the privacy statement
More information:
If, in its privacy statement, and organization claims that only the user has access, and then provides access to someone who is not the user, this breaches the privacy statement.

32. Which of the following statements is most accurate regarding the Children's Online Privacy Protection Act?
D. for websites targeting children 12 years and younger, the Children's Online Privacy Protection Act applies
More information:
The age limit for the Children's Online Privacy Protection Act is under 13, so 12 years and younger.

33. Who publishes and maintains the Federal Communication Commission's official rules?
A. the Government Printing Office
More information:
The Government Printing Office publishes and maintains the Federal Communication Commission's official rules.

34. Which of the following is not one of the four categories of the Fair Information Practices?
A. right of deletion
More information:
The right of deletion is not a category. The other three are.

35. What recommendation would you give as a privacy officer, to prevent leaking personal information?
A. storing data de-identified
More information:
If the data is de-identified, whatever leaks is not personal information anymore.

36. How is the Health Insurance Portability and Accountability Act also known?
C. the Kennedy-Kassebaum Act
More information:
The Health Insurance Portability and Accountability Act is sometimes referred to as the Kennedy-Kassebaum Act. If your study material specifies facts like this try to remember, but don't overdo it as this type of question will likely not form a significant part of the exam.

37. After requesting access, how many days does an organization have to provide a copy of Personal Health Information?
D. thirty days
More information:
When a copy of Personal Health Information is requested from an organization, that organization has thirty days to provide the requested copy.

38. What was the most likely reason for the Confidentiality of Substance Use Disorder Patient Records Rule?
A. to ensure that patients do not face adverse consequences
More information:
Most (if not all) privacy laws are intended to prevent adverse consequences for individuals. The individuals in this case are patients.

39. Which of the following is covered by Title I of the Health Insurance Portability and Accountability Act?
C. workers and their families
More information:
Consult the Health Insurance Portability and Accountability Act for the Titles of the Act. If you are likely going to be needing familiarity with the Health Insurance Portability and Accountability Act beyond your exam this is especially recommended.

40. Which of the following was most likely not a concern with the Health Insurance Portability and Accountability Act?
C. the data security requirements
More information:
The increase in paperwork, penalties and implementation workload have been frequently mentioned as concerns. The data security requirements are not likely a concern with the Health Insurance Portability and Accountability Act.

41. What is most likely true regarding the Health Insurance Portability and Accountability Act in the context of research?
A. there is a decrease in follow-up surveys
More information:
After the implementation of the Health Insurance Portability and Accountability Act there has been a decrease in follow-up surveys.

42. Of the following, which doesn't preempt state law in most areas?
C. the Health Insurance Portability and Accountability Act
More information:
The Health Insurance Portability and Accountability Act does not preempt stricter state law. The others do.

43. What is needed for a potential employer when requesting a consumer report?
B. certifying for permissible purposes
More information:
Certifying that the consumer report will be used for permissible purposes is one of the requirements before a potential employer requests a consumer report.

44. Which of the following requires that debit card numbers are not fully visible?
C. the Fair and Accurate Credit Transaction Act
More information:
The Fair and Accurate Credit Transaction Act requires credit card and debit card numbers not to be fully visible on receipts.

45. Which of the following requires disposal of consumer reports?
C. the disposal rule
More information:
The disposal rule from the Fair and Accurate Credit Transaction Act requires the disposal of a consumer report in a way that prevents unauthorized access.

46. Which is true about the Red Flags Rule?
B. the Red Flags Rule applies to a broad list of businesses
More information:
The Red Flags Rule (a rule to prevent identity theft) applies to financial institutions and creditors, which would be a very broad list.

47. What was the biggest issue in the case of U.S. Bancorp?
C. no actual security issue, but the sharing of customer information
More information:
U.S. Bancorp was accused of selling customer information to telemarketers.

48. Which of the following most accurately describes a criminal trial?
D. liberty and freedom of an individual are at stake
More information:
In a criminal case there is an accusation of being guilty of a crime, leading to a punishment. This is considered to be the liberty and freedom of an individual being at stake.

49. What is the most true about the Family Educational Rights and Privacy Act?
B. state university students must consent to sharing their personal information
More information:
The Family Educational Rights and Privacy Act applies to state funded educational institutions, and the Family Educational Rights and Privacy Act requires students to consent before the educational institutions can share the student's personal information.

50. Which is most true regarding the US National Do Not Call Registry?
A. after your number is on the registry for 31 days, you can report unwanted sales calls
More information:
After your phone number has been on the registry for 31 days, you should not receive unwanted sales calls anymore. If you do receive calls, you can report these.

51. Which Act is complied with, with the Do Not Call Registry?
A. the Do-Not-Call Implementation Act
More information:
It is in the name. There will likely be laws on the exam that are not covered in your study material, so it is recommended to obtain different sources (the internet is always a good option), or in this case take a gamble on the most correct sounding answer.

52. Which of the following is true regarding telemarketing?
B. whenever a call is made, consent must be clear and conspicuous
More information:
The assumption here is that the call is made to someone who is on the Do Not Call Registry, in which case consent is needed. This needs to be clear and conspicuous. See the chapter on telemarketing for the exceptions for telemarketing to persons on the Do Not Call Registry.

53. What is common in most definitions of personal information?
D. it is information about a person
More information:
That the information is about a person is key in personal information.

54. Which of the following is not one of the three basic types of compliance under the Controlling the Assault of Non-Solicited Pornography And Marketing Act?
B. notice compliance
More information:
Notice compliance is not one of the three basic types of compliance under the Controlling the Assault of Non-Solicited Pornography And Marketing Act. The others are.

55. Which state added an explicit guarantee of privacy to its constitution in 1972?
C. California
More information:
The state of California added an explicit guarantee of privacy to its constitution in 1972.

56. Which of the following contains a requirement for the redaction of sensitive personal information?
B. the Federal Rules of Civil Procedure
More information:
The Federal Rules of Civil Procedure contain requirements for the redaction of sensitive personal information to protect the persons involved.

57. Which of the following is not true regarding information in the Federal Rule of Civil Procedure 45?
C. photographic evidence of the receipt of the subpoena is required
More information:
No photographic evidence is required when issuing a subpoena. The other answers are mentioned in the Federal Rule of Civil Procedure 45.

58. Which of the following fits a protective order in the context of personal information?
C. a protective order is often issued to protect against unreasonable discovery requests
More information:
A protection order is often issued against discovery requests. As it can protect all parties, the two answers regarding protecting only one side are incorrect. In addition, even with a protective order information can become known to the public through other sources, regardless of the protective order.

59. How does the Third Amendment provide privacy protection?
B. prevents soldiers from entering a person's home
More information:
The Third Amendment bans soldiers from quartering in a person's home. Although not necessarily relevant currently, it does provide privacy protection.

60. Which of the following is least likely applicable during e-discovery?
B. mandated publication
More information:
There is no publication during e-discovery, only making data available.

61. Which law from 1361 called for the arrest of peeping Toms?
B. the Justices of Peace Act
More information:
The Justices of Peace Act of 131 called for the arrest of peeping Toms.

62. Which of the following was the biggest issue in the Nomi case?
B. Nomi misled customers
More information:
Nomi did not provide everything that was mentioned in their privacy notice, which can be seen as misleading.

63. What can most significantly change the level of privacy protection of an employment at will situation?
A. a contract
More information:
A contract makes privacy agreements enforceable. The others will mostly likely not change the level of privacy as much as a contract could.

64. Of the following, which is the earliest stage of employee privacy protection?
C. consumer reports
More information:
Consumer reports are the first stage where employee privacy protection occurs, following the logic that CCTV is not too invasive and not used for employment purposes.

65. What is created by section 217 of the USA PATRIOT Act?
B. the computer trespasser exception
More information:
The computer trespasser exception was created by section 217 of the USA PATRIOT Act. If you did not know this fact, you could have possibly eliminated the other answers by knowing that they are likely in other Acts and therefore not in the USA PATRIOT Act.

66. What would you recommend as a privacy officer if an organization wants to determine what protection to apply to which data?
B. Data classification
More information:
Data classification allows for classification of a data element, which can include assigning a level of protection.

67. What can be said about comprehensive privacy laws in the US?
D. the privacy laws that do not preempt state law are not comprehensive
More information:
If a law does not preempt state law it is likely not comprehensive, given that a comprehensive law would most likely preempt as it would need to overrule conflicting areas. This is hypothetical and debatable, and the correct answer can be found here by crossing out the more obviously incorrect answers.

68. Which of the following is least likely an incentive for collecting data on employees?
A. European Union legislation in the case of international data transfers
More information:
If anything, the General Data Protection Regulation discourages collecting data on employees.

69. In an international organization, which of the following is most likely true?
A. employees from the European Union seconded in the US could be entitled to the same level of protection as in the European Union
More information:
If an international organization transfers an employee from the European Union to the US, there is a chance that the employee will be under contract in the country of origin, meaning the organization will possibly have to ensure compliance with the General Data Protection Regulation (at work).

70. Which of the following is not true regarding geo-location monitoring by employers in Connecticut?
C. only monitoring practices from a specific exemption list are allowed
More information:
There is no list of exemptions in Connecticut law.

71. Which of the following are partially exempt or not covered under the Employee Polygraph Protection Act?
D. elementary schools
More information:
Elementary schools are not exempt under the Employee Polygraph Protection Act. The others are exempt.

72. Of the following, which is least possibly leading to an obligation to provide personal information?
A. private investigations
More information:
Privately performed investigations do not impose any obligation on the person under investigation to cooperate.

73. In which context was the "reasonable expectation of privacy" test developed?
B. government wiretaps
More information:
This is one of those little facts you can find in your study material.

74. Which of the following was least likely the biggest issue in the snapchat case?
C. snapchat stored passwords non-hashed
More information:
In this case, hackers stole millions of user names and phone numbers and the messages that were only supposed to be visible for a limited amount of time could be stored indefinitely. Storing non-hashed passwords was not part of the case.

75. Which of the following is least likely considered a data breach incident?
C. stolen ciphertext
More information:
Ciphertext is the result of an encryption algorithm. It is data after encryption. Therefore, unless the encryption key is known to the receiver of the ciphertext, this is least likely to be considered a data breach incident, because the stolen data will be useless. Malware is also likely not an issue if the infection occurred on an offline machine, but the chances of that are quite small.

76. Which of the following statements regarding data breaches is least likely true?

B. given its malicious nature, malware always results in a data breach

More information:

If a malware infection occurs on a machine that is not connected to the internet, such as through an infected USB drive, then it is unlikely that the data will be transmitted to the writer of the malware since there is no internet connection to send it through. Therefore, malware does not always result in a data breach.

This case should be used for the following four questions:

A dating website with members all over the world has a unique matching algorithm that matches people based on facial features that have been scientifically proven to result in some form of compatibility. Users consent to the use of facial analysis and the creation of a profile.

Other than for the use of the website, the characteristics of the members that are gathered through the facial scans and conversations with other members, are also used for selling advertisement. Advertisers can buy advertisement space on the website, only visible to a person with a certain profile.

One day, a user is upset with the service, because all her dates have resulted in rejection. The frustration has led her to learn how to hack, and she has breached the website's security and stolen the database with profiles.

77. Which of the following statements is least likely true regarding the part of the dating website hosted in Europe and Hong Kong?
B. for Hong Kong, China's privacy laws are applicable
More information:
In Hong Kong there are privacy laws separate from China. For a brief overview of global privacy laws, read Baker McKenzie's Global Privacy Handbook (free).

78. Which is required for the users from the European Union for the processing of their sexual preference?
C. consent
More information:
A user's sexual preference, regardless of being accurate or not, is considered sensitive personal data. For the processing of sensitive personal data (except for certain exceptions), consent is required.

79. Which of the following is most likely true about storing the political tendencies based on the analysis of someone's face for the members in Europe?
A. constitutes sensitive personal data
More information:
Whether accurate or not, someone's political tendencies can possibly be considered sensitive personal data.

80. If the website is hosted in the European Union, what needs to happen after the breach?
B. the breach needs to be reported to the Data Protection Authority
More information:
Data breaches need to be reported to the Data Protection Authority (within 72 hours).

81. Regarding workplace privacy, and the monitoring of employees, which of the following is closest to being true?
D. there is likely going to be a revision of workplace practices before they can be used in the European branch after a US company buys a company in the European Union
More information:
Given the difference in laws and the future international character of an organization's operations, all laws from the new countries where the activities will take place will have to be respected to the extent that they are applicable. Certain US practices are likely not allowed in Europe, and these practices will need to be adapted to the local situation.

82. Which of the following statements regarding the different branches of government is most accurate?
D. the legislative branch votes on legislation before it is passed
More information:
The legislative branch is made up of the senate and the house (together called congress), who are the ones voting on legislation. Of course the president can vote as well, but from the answers available this is the correct one.

83. If a website claims one thing regarding its processing of personal information, and then does another, what would this likely be called?
B. deceptive practice
More information:
A breach of a promise is a deceptive practice.

84. Which of the following best describes a presidential veto?
D. the ability to say no to a suggestion of congress
More information:
When the president vetoes, he says no to a suggestion of congress.

85. The Fair and Accurate Credit Transactions Act does not help with which of the following?
D. soliciting consumer input
More information:
The persons subject to credit reporting are not required by the Fair and Accurate Credit Transactions Act to provide input.

86. When looking at the privacy laws in Canada, Europe and Asia, which class of privacy is most comprehensively protected?
C. information privacy
More information:
This question should be easy, as you are mostly reading about personal INFORMATION.

87. When looking at the Fair Information Practices, which of the following is not one of them?
D. supervision
More information:
Supervision is not one of the principles.

88. Which of the following is true about robocalls?
B. they are prerecorded
More information:
Although there are many different conceptions of what constitutes a robocall, your study material claims it is a prerecorded call.

89. What cannot be said about common law?
A. it requires privacy torts
More information:
There can be common law without privacy torts. They help, because it adds to common law, but it is not required.

90. When would a privacy officer most likely recommend informing people of an updated privacy notice?
C. when personal information will be handled differently
More information:
When personal information is going to be handled differently, this is what users would likely need to be informed of so they can take action according to their wishes based on the new situation.

www.ingramcontent.com/pod-product-compliance
Lightning Source LLC
Chambersburg PA
CBHW030532220526